The Vibrant Diabetic Diet Side Dish Cooking Book

Give a Better Taste to Your Siders with These Quick and Easy
Recipes for Beginners

Rachel Holmes

contained within this document, including, but not limited to, — errors, omissions, or inaccuracies.

Table of contents

Quinoa Tabbouleh

Preparation Time : 8 minutes

Cooking Time : 16 minutes

Servings : 6

Ingredients :

- 1 cup quinoa, rinsed
- 1 large English cucumber
- 2 scallions, sliced
- 2 cups cherry tomatoes, halved
- 2/3 cup chopped parsley
- 1/2 cup chopped mint
- ½ teaspoon minced garlic
- 1/2 teaspoon salt
- ½ teaspoon ground black pepper
- 2 tablespoon lemon juice
- 1/2 cup olive oil

Directions :

1. Plugin Pressure Pot, insert the inner pot, add quinoa, then pour in water and stir until mixed.

2. Close Pressure Pot with its lid and turn the pressure knob to seal the pot.

3. Select 'manual' button, then set the 'timer' to 1 minute and cook in high pressure, it may take 7 minutes.

4. Once the timer stops, select 'cancel' button and do natural pressure release for 10 minutes and then do quick pressure release until pressure nob drops down.

5. Open the Pressure Pot, fluff quinoa with a fork, then spoon it on a rimmed baking sheet, spread quinoa evenly and let cool.

6. Meanwhile, place lime juice in a small bowl, add garlic and stir until just mixed.

7. Then add salt, black pepper, and olive oil and whisk until combined.

8. Transfer cooled quinoa to a large bowl, add remaining ingredients, then drizzle generously with the prepared lime juice mixture and toss until evenly coated.

9. Taste quinoa to adjust seasoning and then serve.

Nutrition : 283 Calories; 30.6g Carbohydrates; 3.4g Fiber

Wild Rice Salad with Cranberries and Almonds

Preparation Time : 6 minutes

Cooking Time : 25 minutes

Servings : 18

Ingredients :

For the rice

- 2 cups wild rice blend, rinsed
- 1 teaspoon kosher salt
- 2½ cups Vegetable Broth

For the dressing

- ¼ cup extra-virgin olive oil
- ¼ cup white wine vinegar
- 1½ teaspoons grated orange zest
- Juice of 1 medium orange (about ¼ cup)
- 1 teaspoon honey or pure maple syrup

For the salad

- ¾ cup unsweetened dried cranberries
- ½ cup sliced almonds, toasted
- Freshly ground black pepper

Directions :

1. To make the rice
2. In the electric pressure cooker, combine the rice, salt, and broth.
3. Close and lock the lid. Set the valve to sealing.

4. Cook on high pressure for 25 minutes.

5. When the cooking is complete, hit Cancel and allow the pressure to release naturally for 1minutes, then quick release any remaining pressure.

6. Once the pin drops, unlock and remove the lid.

7. Let the rice cool briefly, then fluff it with a fork.

8. To make the dressing

9. While the rice cooks, make the dressing: In a small jar with a screw-top lid, combine the olive oil, vinegar, zest, juice, and honey. (If you don't have a jar, whisk the ingredients together in a small bowl.) Shake to combine.

10. To make the salad

11. Mix rice, cranberries, and almonds.

12. Add the dressing and season with pepper.

13. Serve warm or refrigerate.

Nutrition: 126 Calories; 18g Carbohydrates; 2g Fiber

Low Fat Roasties

Preparation Time : 8 minutes

Cooking Time : 25 minutes

Servings : 2

Ingredients:

- 1lb roasting potatoes
- 1 garlic clove
- 1 cup vegetable stock
- 2tbsp olive oil

Directions :

1. Position potatoes in the steamer basket and add the stock into the Pressure Pot.

2. Steam the potatoes in your Pressure Pot for 15 minutes.

3. Depressurize and pour away the remaining stock.

4. Set to sauté and add the oil, garlic, and potatoes. Cook until brown.

Nutrition : 201 Calories; 3g Carbohydrates; 6g Fat

Roasted Parsnips

Preparation Time : 9 minutes

Cooking Time : 25 minutes

Servings : 2

Ingredients :

- 1lb parsnips
- 1 cup vegetable stock
- 2tbsp herbs
- 2tbsp olive oil

Directions:

1. Put the parsnips in the steamer basket and add the stock into the Pressure Pot.

2. Steam the parsnips in your Pressure Pot for 15 minutes.

3. Depressurize and pour away the remaining stock.

4. Set to sauté and add the oil, herbs and parsnips.

5. Cook until golden and crisp.

Nutrition : 130 Calories; 14g Carbohydrates; 4g Protein

Lower Carb Hummus

Preparation Time : 9 minutes

Cooking Time : 60 minutes

Servings : 2

Ingredients :

- 0.5 cup dry chickpeas
- 1 cup vegetable stock
- 1 cup pumpkin puree
- 2tbsp smoked paprika
- salt and pepper to taste

Directions :

1. Soak the chickpeas overnight.
2. Place the chickpeas and stock in the Pressure Pot.
3. Cook on Beans 60 minutes.
4. Depressurize naturally.
5. Blend the chickpeas with the remaining ingredients.

Nutrition : 135 Calories; 18g Carbohydrates; 3g Fat

Sweet and Sour Red Cabbage

Preparation Time : 7 minutes

Cooking Time : 10 minutes

Servings : 8

Ingredients :

- 2 cups Spiced Pear Applesauce
- 1 small onion, chopped
- ½ cup apple cider vinegar
- ½ teaspoon kosher salt
- 1 head red cabbage

Directions :

1. In the electric pressure cooker, combine the applesauce, onion, vinegar, salt, and cup of water. Stir in the cabbage.
2. Seal lid of the pressure cooker.
3. Cook on high pressure for 10 minutes.
4. When the cooking is complete, hit Cancel and quick release the pressure.
5. Once the pin drops, unlock and remove the lid.
6. Spoon into a bowl or platter and serve.

Nutrition : 91 Calories; 18g Carbohydrates; 4g Fiber

Pinto Beans

Preparation Time : 6 minutes

Cooking Time : 55 minutes

Servings : 10

Ingredients :

- 2 cups pinto beans, dried
- 1 medium white onion
- 1 ½ teaspoon minced garlic
- ¾ teaspoon salt
- 1/4 teaspoon ground black pepper
- 1 teaspoon red chili powder
- 1/4 teaspoon cumin
- 1 tablespoon olive oil
- 1 teaspoon chopped cilantro
- 5 ½ cup vegetable stock

Directions :

1. Plugin Pressure Pot, insert the inner pot, press sauté/simmer button, add oil and when hot, add onion and garlic and cook for 3 minutes or until onions begin to soften.

2. Add remaining ingredients, stir well, then press the cancel button, shut the Pressure Pot with its lid and seal the pot.

3. Click 'manual' button, then press the 'timer' to set the cooking time to 45 minutes and cook at high pressure.

4. Once done, click 'cancel' button and do natural pressure release for 10 minutes until pressure nob drops down.

5. Open the Pressure Pot, spoon beans into plates and serve.

Nutrition : 107 Calories; 11.7g Carbohydrates; 4g Fiber

Parmesan Cauliflower Mash

Preparation Time : 19 minutes

Cooking Time : 5 minutes

Servings : 4

Ingredients:

- 1 head cauliflower
- ½ teaspoon kosher salt
- ½ teaspoon garlic pepper
- 2 tablespoons plain Greek yogurt
- ¾ cup freshly grated Parmesan cheese
- 1 tablespoon unsalted butter or ghee (optional)
- Chopped fresh chives

Directions :

1. Pour cup of water into the electric pressure cooker and insert a steamer basket or wire rack.
2. Place the cauliflower in the basket.
3. Cover lid of the pressure cooker to seal.
4. Cook on high pressure for 5 minutes.
5. Once complete, hit Cancel and quick release the pressure.
6. When the pin drops, remove the lid.
7. Remove the cauliflower from the pot and pour out the water. Return the cauliflower to the pot and add the salt, garlic pepper, yogurt, and cheese. Use an immersion blender to purée or mash the cauliflower in the pot.

8. Spoon into a serving bowl, and garnish with butter (if using) and chives.

Nutrition : 141 Calories; 12g Carbohydrates;4g Fiber

Steamed Asparagus

Preparation Time : 3 minutes

Cooking Time : 2 minutes

Servings : 4

Ingredients:

- 1 lb. fresh asparagus, rinsed and tough ends trimmed
- 1 cup water

Directions :

1. Place the asparagus into a wire steamer rack, and set it inside your Pressure Pot.

2. Add water to the pot. Close and seal the lid, turning the steam release valve to the "Sealing" position.

3. Select the "Steam" function to cook on high pressure for 2 minutes.

4. Once done, do a quick pressure release of the steam.

5. Lift the wire steamer basket out of the pot and place the asparagus onto a serving plate.

6. Season as desired and serve.

Nutrition : 22 Calories; 4g Carbohydrates; 2g Protein

Squash Medley

Preparation Time : 10 minutes

Cooking Time : 20 minutes.

Servings : 2

Ingredients :

- 2 lbs. mixed squash
- ½ cup mixed veg
- 1 cup vegetable stock
- 2 tbsps. olive oil
- 2 tbsps. mixed herbs

Directions :

1. Put the squash in the steamer basket and add the stock into the Pressure Pot.
2. Steam the squash in your Pressure Pot for 10 minutes.
3. Depressurize and pour away the remaining stock.
4. Set to sauté and add the oil and remaining ingredients.
5. Cook until a light crust form.

Nutrition : 100 Calories; 10g Carbohydrates; 6g Fat

Eggplant Curry

Preparation Time : 15 minutes

Cooking Time : 20 minutes

Servings : 2

Ingredients :

- 3 cups chopped eggplant
- 1 thinly sliced onion
- 1 cup coconut milk
- 3 tbsps. curry paste
- 1 tbsp. oil or ghee

Directions:

1. Select Pressure Pot to sauté and put the onion, oil, and curry paste.

2. Once the onion is soft, stir in remaining ingredients and seal.

3. Cook on Stew for 20 minutes. Release the pressure naturally.

Nutrition : 350 Calories; 15g Carbohydrates; 25g Fat

Lentil and Eggplant Stew

Preparation Time : 15 minutes

Cooking Time : 35 minutes

Servings : 2

Ingredients :

- 1 lb. eggplant
- 1 lb. dry lentils
- 1 cup chopped vegetables
- 1 cup low sodium vegetable broth

Directions :

1. Incorporate all the ingredients in your Pressure Pot, cook on Stew for 35 minutes.

2. Release the pressure naturally and serve.

Nutrition : 310 Calories; 22g Carbohydrates; 10g Fat

Tofu Curry

Preparation Time : 15 minutes

Cooking Time : 20 minutes

Servings : 2

Ingredients :

- 2 cups cubed extra firm tofu
- 2 cups mixed stir fry vegetables
- ½ cup soy yogurt
- 3 tbsps. curry paste
- 1 tbsp. oil or ghee

Directions :

1. Set the Pressure Pot to sauté and add the oil and curry paste.
2. Once soft, place the remaining ingredients except for the yogurt and seal.
3. Cook on Stew for 20 minutes.
4. Release the pressure naturally and serve with a scoop of soy yogurt.

Nutrition : 300 Calories; 9g Carbohydrates; 14g Fat

Lentil and Chickpea Curry

Preparation Time : 15 minutes

Cooking Time : 20 minutes

Servings : 2

Ingredients :

- 2 cups dry lentils and chickpeas
- 1 thinly sliced onion
- 1 cup chopped tomato
- 3 tbsps. curry paste
- 1 tbsp. oil or ghee

Directions :

1. Press Pressure Pot to sauté and mix onion, oil, and curry paste.
2. Once the onion is cooked, stir the remaining ingredients and seal.
3. Cook on Stew for 20 minutes.
4. Release the pressure naturally and serve.

Nutrition: 360 Calories; 26g Carbohydrates; 19g Fat

Split Pea Stew

Preparation Time : 5 minutes

Cooking Time : 35 minutes

Servings : 2

Ingredients :

- 1 cup dry split peas
- 1 lb. chopped vegetables
- 1 cup mushroom soup
- 2 tbsps. old bay seasoning

Directions :

1. Incorporate all the ingredients in Pressure Pot, cook for 33 minutes.
2. Release the pressure naturally.

Nutrition : 300 Calories; 7g Carbohydrates; 2g Fat

Fried Tofu Hotpot

Preparation Time : 15 minutes

Cooking Time : 15 minutes

Servings : 2

Ingredients :

- ½ lb. fried tofu
- 1 lb. chopped Chinese vegetable mix
- 1 cup low sodium vegetable broth
- 2 tbsps. 5 spice seasoning
- 1 tbsp. smoked paprika

Directions :

1. Combine all the ingredients in your Pressure Pot, set on Stew for 15 minutes.
2. Release the pressure naturally and serve.

Nutrition : 320 Calories; 11g Carbohydrates; 23g Fat

Chili Sin Carne

Preparation Time : 15 minutes

Cooking Time : 35 minutes

Servings : 2

Ingredients :

- 3 cups mixed cooked beans
- 2 cups chopped tomatoes
- 1 tbsp. yeast extract
- 2 squares very dark chocolate
- 1 tbsp. red chili flakes

Directions :

1. Combine all the ingredients in your Pressure Pot, cook for 35 minutes.
2. Release the pressure naturally and serve.

Nutrition : 240 Calories; 20g Carbohydrates; 3g Fat

Chick Pea and Kale Dish

Preparation Time : 10 minutes

Cooking Time : 25-30 minutes

Servings :4

Ingredients :

- 2 cups chickpea flour
- 1/2 cup green bell pepper, diced
- 1/2 cup onions, minced
- 1 tablespoon oregano
- 1 tablespoon salt
- 1 teaspoon cayenne
- 4 cups spring water
- 2 tablespoons Grape Seed Oil

Directions :

1. Boil spring water in a large pot
2. Lower heat into medium and whisk in chickpea flour
3. Add some minced onions, diced green bell pepper, seasoning to the pot and cook for 10 minutes
4. Cover dish using a baking sheet, grease with oil
5. Pour batter into the sheet and spread with a spatula
6. Cover with another sheet
7. Transfer to a fridge and chill, for 20 minutes
8. Remove from freezer and cut batter into fry shapes
9. Preheat the Air Fryer, to 385 degrees F

10. Transfer fries into the cooking basket, lightly greased and cover with parchment

11. Bake for about 15 minutes, flip and bake for 10 minutes more until golden brown

12. Serve and enjoy!

Nutrition : Calories: 271 kcal; Carbohydrates: 28 g; Fat: 15 g; Protein: 9 g

Zucchini Chips

Preparation Time : *10 minutes*

Cooking Time : *12-15 minutes*

Servings :4

Ingredients :

- *Salt as needed*
- *Grape seed oil as needed*
- *6 zucchinis*

Directions :

1. Into 330 F, pre heat the Air Fryer
2. Wash zucchini, slice zucchini into thin strips
3. Put slices in a bowl and add oil, salt, and toss
4. Spread over the cooking basket, fry for 12-15 minutes
5. Serve and enjoy!

Nutrition : Calories: 92 kcal; Carbohydrates: 6 g;Fat: 7 g; Protein: 2 g

Classic Blueberry Spelt Muffins

Preparation Time : 10 minutes

Cooking Time : 12-15 minutes

Servings :4

Ingredients :

- 1/4 sea salt
- 1/3 cup maple syrup
- 1 teaspoon baking powder
- 1/2 cup sea moss
- 3/4 cup spelt flour
- 3/4 cup Kamut flour
- 1 cup hemp milk
- 1 cup blueberries

Directions :

1. Into 380 degrees F pre heat Air Fryer
2. Take your muffin tins and gently grease them
3. Take a bowl and add flour, syrup, salt, baking powder, seamless and mix well
4. Add milk and mix well
5. Fold in blueberries
6. Pour into muffin tins
7. Transfer to the cooking basket, bake for 20-25 minutes until nicely baked
8. Serve and enjoy!

Nutrition : Calories: 217 kcal; Carbohydrates: 32 g; Fat: 9 g;
Protein: 4 g

Genuine Healthy Crackers

Preparation Time : 10 minutes

Cooking Time : 12-15 minutes

Servings :4

Ingredients :

- 1/2 cup Rye flour
- 1 cup spelt flour
- 2 teaspoons sesame seed
- 1 teaspoon agave syrup
- 1 teaspoon salt
- 2 tablespoons grapeseed oil
- 3/4 cup spring water

Directions :

1. Into 330 degrees F, Preheat the Air Fryer
2. Take a medium bowl and add all Ingredients, mix well
3. Make dough ball
4. Prepare a place for rolling out the dough, cover with a piece of parchment
5. Lightly grease paper with grape seed oil, place dough
6. Roll out, dough with a rolling pin, add more flour if needed
7. Take a shape cutter and cut dough into squares
8. Place squares in Air Fryer cooking basket
9. Brush with more oil

10. Sprinkle salt

11. Bake for 10-15 minutes until golden

12. Let it cool, serve, and enjoy!

Nutrition : Calories: 226 kcal; Carbohydrates: 41 g; Fat: 3 g; Protein: 11 g

Tortilla Chips

Preparation Time : 10 minutes

Cooking Time : 8-12 minutes

Servings : 4

Ingredients :

- 2 cups of spelt flour
- 1 teaspoon of salt
- 1/2 cup of spring water
- 1/3 cup of grapeseed oil

Directions :

1. Preheat your Air Fryer into 320 degrees F
2. Take the food processor then add salt, flour, and process well for 15 seconds
3. Gradually add grapeseed oil until mixed
4. Keep mixing until you have a nice dough
5. Formulate work surface and cover in a piece of parchment, sprinkle flour
6. Knead the dough for 1-2 minutes
7. Grease cooking basket with oil
8. Transfer dough on the cooking basket, brush oil and sprinkle salt
9. Cut dough into 8 triangles
10. Bake for about 8-12 minutes until golden brown
11. Serve and enjoy once done!

Nutrition : Calories: 288 kcal; Carbohydrates: 18 g; Fat: 17 g;
Protein: 16 g

Pumpkin Spice Crackers

Preparation Time : 10 minutes

Cooking Time : 60 minutes

Servings : 6

Ingredients :

- 1/3 cup coconut flour
- 2 tablespoons pumpkin pie spice
- ¾ cup sunflower seeds
- ¾ cup flaxseed
- 1/3 cup sesame seeds
- 1 tablespoon ground psyllium husk powder
- 1 teaspoon sea salt
- 3 tablespoons coconut oil, melted
- 11/3 cups alkaline water

Directions :

1. Set your oven to 300 degrees F.
2. Combine all dry Ingredients in a bowl.
3. Add water and oil to the mixture and mix well.
4. Let the dough stay for 2 to 3 minutes.

5. Spread the dough evenly on a cookie sheet lined with parchment paper.

6. Bake for 30 minutes.

7. Reduce the oven heat to low and bake for another 30 minutes.

8. Crack the bread into bite-size pieces.

9. Serve

Nutrition : Calories 248; Total Fat 15.7 g; Saturated Fat 2.7 g; Cholesterol 75 mg; Sodium 94 mg; Total Carbs 0.4 g; Fiber 0g; Sugar 0 g; Protein 24.9 g

Spicy Roasted Nuts

Preparation Time : 10 minutes

Cooking Time : 15 minutes

Servings : 4

Ingredients :

- 8 oz. pecans or almonds or walnuts
- 1 teaspoon sea salt
- 1 tablespoon olive oil or coconut oil
- 1 teaspoon ground cumin
- 1 teaspoon paprika powder or chili powder

Directions :

1. Add all the Ingredients to a skillet.
2. Roast the nuts until golden brown.
3. Serve and enjoy.

Nutrition : Calories 287; Total Fat 29.5 g; Saturated Fat 3 g; Cholesterol 0 mg; Total Carbs 5.9 g; Sugar 1.4g; Fiber 4.3 g; Sodium 388 mg; Protein 4.2 g

Wheat Crackers

Preparation Time : 10 minutes

Cooking Time : 20 minutes

Servings : 4

Ingredients :

- 1 3/4 cups almond flour
- 1 1/2 cups coconut flour
- 3/4 teaspoon sea salt
- 1/3 cup vegetable oil
- 1 cup alkaline water
- Sea salt for sprinkling

Directions :

1. Set your oven to 350 degrees F.
2. Mix coconut flour, almond flour and salt in a bowl.
3. Stir in vegetable oil and water. Mix well until smooth.
4. Spread this dough on a floured surface into a thin sheet.
5. Cut small squares out of this sheet.
6. Arrange the dough squares on a baking sheet lined with parchment paper.
7. For about 20 minutes, bake until light golden in color.
8. Serve.

Nutrition : Calories 64; Total Fat 9.2 g; Saturated Fat 2.4 g; Cholesterol 110 mg; Sodium 276 mg; Total Carbs 9.2 g; Fiber 0.9 g; Sugar 1.4 g; Protein 1.5 g

Potato Chips

Preparation Time : 10 minutes

Cooking Time : 20 minutes

Servings : 4

Ingredients :

- 1 tablespoon vegetable oil

- 1 potato, sliced paper thin

- Sea salt, to taste

Directions :

1. Toss potato with oil and sea salt.

2. Spread the slices in a baking dish in a single layer.

3. Cook in a microwave for 5 minutes until golden brown.

4. Serve.

Nutrition : Calories 80; Total Fat 3.5 g; Saturated Fat 0.1 g; Cholesterol 320 mg; Sodium 350 mg; Total Carbs 11.6 g; Fiber 0.7 g; Sugar 0.7 g; Protein 1.2 g

Zucchini Pepper Chips

Preparation Time : 10 minutes

Cooking Time : 15 minutes

Servings : 4

Ingredients :

- 1 2/3 cups vegetable oil
- 1 teaspoon garlic powder
- 1 teaspoon onion powder
- 1/2 teaspoon black pepper
- 3 tablespoons crushed red pepper flakes
- 2 zucchinis, thinly sliced

Directions :

1. Mix oil with all the spices in a bowl.
2. Add zucchini slices and mix well.
3. Transfer the mixture to a Ziplock bag and seal it.
4. Refrigerate for 10 minutes.
5. Spread the zucchini slices on a greased baking sheet.
6. Bake for 15 minutes
7. Serve.

Nutrition : Calories 172; Total Fat 11.1 g; Saturated Fat 5.8 g; Cholesterol 610 mg; Sodium 749 mg; Total Carbs 19.9 g; Fiber 0.2 g; Sugar 0.2 g; Protein 13.5 g

Apple Chips

Preparation Time : 5 minutes

Cooking Time : 45 minutes

Servings :4

Ingredients :

- 2 Golden Delicious apples, cored and thinly sliced
- 1 1/2 teaspoons white sugar
- 1/2 teaspoon ground cinnamon

Directions :

1. Set your oven to 225 degrees F.
2. Place apple slices on a baking sheet.
3. Sprinkle sugar an
4. d cinnamon over apple slices.
5. Bake for 45 minutes.
6. Serve

Nutrition : Calories 127; Total Fat 3.5 g; Saturated Fat 0.5 g; Cholesterol 162 mg; Sodium 142 mg; Total Carbs 33.6g; Fiber 0.4 g; Sugar 0.5 g; Protein 4.5 g

Kale Crisps

Preparation Time : 10 minutes

Cooking Time : 10 minutes

Servings : 4

Ingredients :

- 1 bunch kale, remove the stems, leaves torn into even pieces
- 1 tablespoon olive oil
- 1 teaspoon sea salt

Directions :

1. Set your oven to 350 degrees F. Layer a baking sheet with parchment paper.
2. Spread the kale leaves on a paper towel to absorb all the moisture.
3. Toss the leaves with sea salt, and olive oil.
4. Kindly spread them, on the baking sheet and bake for 10 minutes.
5. Serve.

Nutrition : Calories 113; Total Fat 7.5 g; Saturated Fat 1.1 g; Cholesterol 20 mg; Sodium 97 mg; Total Carbs 1.4 g; Fiber 0 g; Sugar 0 g; Protein 1.1g

Carrot Chips

Preparation Time : 5 minutes

Cooking Time : 12 minutes

Servings : 4

Ingredients :

- 4 carrots, washed, peeled and sliced
- 2 teaspoons extra-virgin olive oil
- 1/4 teaspoon sea salt

Directions :

1. Set your oven to 350 degrees F.
2. Toss carrots with salt and olive oil.
3. Spread the slices into two baking sheets in a single layer.
4. Bake for 6 minutes on upper and lower rack of the oven.
5. Switch the baking racks and bake for another 6 minutes.
6. Serve.

Nutrition : Calories 153; Total Fat 7.5 g; Saturated Fat 1.1 g; Cholesterol 20 mg; Sodium 97 mg; Total Carbs 20.4 g; Fiber 0 g; Sugar 0 g; Protein 3.1g

Pita Chips

Preparation Time : 5 minutes

Cooking Time : 12 minutes

Servings : 4

Ingredients :

- 12 pita bread pockets, sliced into triangles
- 1/2 cup olive oil
- 1/2 teaspoon ground black pepper
- 1 teaspoon garlic salt
- 1/2 teaspoon dried basil
- 1 teaspoon dried chervil

Directions :

1. Set your oven to 400 degrees F.
2. Toss pita with all the remaining Ingredients in a bowl.
3. Spread the seasoned triangles on a baking sheet.
4. Bake for 7 minutes until golden brown.
5. Serve with your favorite hummus.

Nutrition : Calories 201; Total Fat 5.5 g; Saturated Fat 2.1 g; Cholesterol 10 mg; Sodium 597 mg; Total Carbs 2.4 g; Fiber 0 g; Sugar 0 g; Protein 3.1g

Sweet Potato Chips

Preparation Time : 5 minutes

Cooking Time : 5 minutes

Servings : 4

Ingredients :

- 1 sweet potato, thinly sliced
- 2 teaspoons olive oil, or as needed
- Coarse sea salt, to taste

Directions :

1. Toss sweet potato with oil and salt.
2. Spread the slices in a baking dish in a single layer.
3. Cook in a microwave for 5 minutes until golden brown.
4. Serve.

Nutrition : Calories 213; Total Fat 8.5 g; Saturated Fat 3.1 g; Cholesterol 120 mg; Sodium 497 mg; Total Carbs 21.4 g; Fiber 0 g; Sugar 0 g; Protein 0.1g

Spinach and Sesame Crackers

Preparation Time : 5 minutes

Cooking Time : 15 minutes

Servings : 4

Ingredients :

- 2 tablespoons white sesame seeds
- 1 cup fresh spinach, washed
- 1 2/3 cups all-purpose flour
- 1/2 cup water
- 1/2 teaspoon baking powder
- 1 teaspoon olive oil
- 1 teaspoon salt

Directions :

1. Transfer the spinach to a blender with a half cup water and blend until smooth.

2. Add 2 tablespoons white sesame seeds, ½ teaspoon baking powder, 1 2/3 cups all-purpose flour, and 1 teaspoon salt to a bowl and stir well until combined. Add in 1 teaspoon olive oil and spinach water. Mix again and knead by using your hands until you obtain a smooth dough.

3. If the made dough is too gluey, then add more flour.

4. Using your parchment paper lightly roll out the dough as thin as possible. Cut into squares with a pizza cutter.

5. Bake into a preheated oven at 400°, for about 15to 20 minutes. Once done, let cool and then serve.

Nutrition : 223 Calories; 3g Fat; 41g Total Carbohydrates; 6g Protein

Mini Nacho Pizzas

Preparation Time : 5 minutes

Cooking Time : 10 minutes

Servings : 4

Ingredients :

- 1/4 cup refried beans, vegan
- 2 tablespoons tomato, diced
- 2 English muffins, split in half
- 1/4 cup onion, sliced
- 1/3 cup vegan cheese, shredded
- 1 small jalapeno, sliced
- 1/3 cup roasted tomato salsa
- 1/2 avocado, diced and tossed in lemon juice

Directions :

1. Add the refried beans/salsa onto the muffin bread. Sprinkle with shredded vegan cheese followed by the veggie toppings.

2. Transfer to a baking sheet and place in a preheated oven at 350 to 400 F on a top rack.

3. Put into the oven for 10 minutes and then broil for 2minutes, so that the top becomes bubbly.

4. Take out from the oven and let them cool at room temperature.

5. Top with avocado. Enjoy!

Nutrition : 133 Calories; 4.2g Fat; 719g Total Carbohydrates; 6g Protein

Pizza Sticks

Preparation Time : 10 minutes

Cooking Time : 30 minutes

Servings : 16 sticks

Ingredients :

- 5 tablespoons tomato sauce
- Few pinches of dried basil
- 1 block extra firm tofu
- 2 tablespoon + 2 teaspoon Nutritional yeast

Directions :

1. Cape the tofu in a paper tissue and put a cutting board on top, place something heavy on top and drain for about 10 to 15 minutes.

2. In the meantime, line your baking sheet with parchment paper. Cut the tofu into 16 equal pieces and place them on a baking sheet.

3. Spread each pizza stick with a teaspoon of marinara sauce.

4. Sprinkle each stick with half teaspoon of yeast, followed by basil on top.

5. Bake into a preheated oven at 425 F for about 28 to 30 minutes. Serve and enjoy!

Nutrition :33 Calories; 1.7g Fat; 2g Total Carbs; 3g Protein

Raw Broccoli Poppers

Preparation Time : 2 minutes

Cooking Time : 8 minutes

Servings: 4

Ingredients :

- 1/8 cup water
- 1/8 teaspoon fine sea salt
- 4 cups broccoli florets, washed and cut into 1-inch pieces
- 1/4 teaspoon turmeric powder
- 1 cup unsalted cashews, soaked overnight or at least 3-4 hours and drained
- 1/4 teaspoon onion powder
- 1 red bell pepper, seeded and
- 2 heaping tablespoons Nutritional
- 2 tablespoons lemon juice

Directions :

1. Transfer the drained cashews to a high-speed blender and pulse for about 30 seconds. Add in the chopped pepper and pulse again for 30seconds.

2. Add some 2 tablespoons lemon juice, 1/8 cup water, 2heaping tablespoons Nutritional yeast, ¼ teaspoon onion powder, 1/8 teaspoon fine sea salt, and 1/4 teaspoon turmeric powder. Pulse for about 45 seconds until smooth.

3. Handover the broccoli into a bowl and add in chopped cheesy cashew mixture. Toss well until coated.

4. Transfer the pieces of broccoli to the trays of a yeast dehydrator.

5. Follow the dehydrator's instructions and dehydrate for about 8 minutes at 125 F or until crunchy.

Nutrition : 408 Calories; 32g Fat; 22g Total Carbohydrates; 15g Protein

Blueberry Cauliflower

Preparation Time : 2 minutes

Cooking Time : 5 minutes

Servings : 1

Ingredients :

- ¼ cup frozen strawberries
- 2 teaspoons maple syrup
- ¾ cup unsweetened cashew milk
- 1 teaspoon vanilla extract
- ½ cup plain cashew yogurt
- 5 tablespoons powdered peanut butter
- ¾ cup frozen wild blueberries
- ½ cup cauliflower florets, coarsely chopped

Directions :

1. Add all the smoothie Ingredients to a high-speed blender.
2. Blitz to combine until smooth.
3. Pour into a chilled glass and serve.

Nutrition : 340 Calories; 11g Fat; 48g Total Carbohydrates; 16g Protein

Candied Ginger

Preparation Time : 10 minutes

Cooking Time : 40 minutes

Servings : 3 to 5

Ingredients :

- 2 1/2 cups salted pistachios, shelled
- 1 1/4 teaspoons powdered ginger
- 3 tablespoons pure maple syrup

Directions :

1. Add 1 1/4 teaspoons powdered ginger to a bowl with pistachios. Stir well until combined. There

2. should be no lumps.

3. Drizzle with 3 tablespoons of maple syrup and stir well.

4. Transfer to a baking sheet lined with parchment paper and spread evenly.

5. Cook into a preheated oven at 275 F for about 20 minutes.

6. Take out from oven, stir, and cook for further 10 to 15 minutes.

7. Let it cool for about few minutes until crispy. Enjoy!

Nutrition : 378 Calories; 27.6g Fat; 26g Total Carbohydrates; 13g Protein

Brussels Sprouts

Preparation Time : 5 minutes

Cooking Time : 3 minutes

Servings : 5

Ingredients :

- 1 tsp. extra-virgin olive oil
- 1 lb. halved Brussels sprouts
- 3 tbsps. apple cider vinegar
- 3 tbsps. gluten-free tamari soy sauce
- 3 tbsps. chopped sun-dried tomatoes

Directions :

1. Select the "Sauté" function on your Pressure Pot, add oil and allow the pot to get hot.

2. Cancel the "Sauté" function and add the Brussels sprouts.

3. Stir well and allow the sprouts to cook in the residual heat for 2-3 minutes.

4. Add the tamari soy sauce and vinegar, and then stir.

5. Cover the Pressure Pot, sealing the pressure valve by pointing it to "Sealing."

6. Select the "Manual, High Pressure" setting and cook for 3 minutes.

7. Once the cook cycle is done, do a quick pressure release, and then stir in the chopped sun-dried tomatoes.

8. Serve immediately.

Nutrition : 62 Calories; 10g Carbohydrates; 1g Fat

Garlic and Herb Carrots

Preparation Time : 2 minutes

Cooking Time : 18 minutes

Servings : 3

Ingredients :

- 2 tbsps. butter
- 1 lb. baby carrots
- 1 cup water
- 1 tsp. fresh thyme or oregano
- 1 tsp. minced garlic
- Black pepper
- Coarse sea salt

Directions :

1. Fill water to the inner pot of the Pressure Pot, and then put in a steamer basket.

2. Layer the carrots into the steamer basket.

3. Close and seal the lid, with the pressure vent in the "Sealing" position.

4. Select the "Steam" setting and cook for 2 minutes on high pressure.

5. Quick release the pressure and then carefully remove the steamer basket with the steamed carrots, discarding the water.

6. Add butter to the inner pot of the Pressure Pot and allow it to melt on the "Sauté" function.

7. Add garlic and sauté for 30 seconds, and then add the carrots. Mix well.

8. Stir in the fresh herbs, and cook for 2-3 minutes.

9. Season with salt and black pepper, and the transfer to a serving bowl.

10. Serve warm and enjoy!

Nutrition : 122 Calories; 12g Carbohydrates; 7g Fat

Cilantro Lime Drumsticks

Preparation Time : 5 minutes

Cooking Time : 15 minutes

Servings : 6

Ingredients :

- 1 tbsp. olive oil
- 6 chicken drumsticks
- 4 minced garlic cloves
- ½ cup low-sodium chicken broth
- 1 tsp. cayenne pepper
- 1 tsp. crushed red peppers
- 1 tsp. fine sea salt
- Juice of 1 lime

To Serve:

- 2 tbsp. chopped cilantro
- Extra lime zest

Directions:

1. Pour olive oil to the Pressure Pot and set it on the "Sauté" function.

2. Once the oil is hot adding the chicken drumsticks, and season them well.

3. Using tongs, stir the drumsticks and brown the drumsticks for 2 minutes per side.

4. Add the lime juice, fresh cilantro, and chicken broth to the pot.

5. Lock and seal the lid, turning the pressure valve to "Sealing."

6. Cook the drumsticks on the "Manual, High Pressure" setting for 9 minutes.

7. Once done let the pressure release naturally.

8. Carefully transfer the drumsticks to an aluminum-foiled baking sheet and broil them in the oven for 3-5 minutes until golden brown.

9. Serve warm, garnished with more cilantro and lime zest.

Nutrition : 480 Calories; 3.3g Carbohydrates; 29g Fat

Eggplant Spread

Preparation Time : 5 minutes

Cooking Time : 18 minutes

Servings : 5

Ingredients :

- 4 tbsps. extra-virgin olive oil
- 2 lbs. eggplant
- 4 skin-on garlic cloves
- ½ cup water
- ¼ cup pitted black olives
- 3 sprigs fresh thyme
- Juice of 1 lemon
- 1 tbsp. tahini
- 1 tsp. sea salt
- Fresh extra-virgin olive oil

Directions :

1. Peel the eggplant in alternating stripes, leaving some areas with skin and some with no skin.

2. Slice into big chunks and layer at the bottom of your Pressure Pot.

3. Add olive oil to the pot, and on the "Sauté" function, fry and caramelize the eggplant on one side, about 5 minutes.

4. Add in the garlic cloves with the skin on.

5. Flip over the eggplant and then add in the remaining uncooked eggplant chunks, salt, and water.

6. Close the lid, ensure the pressure release valve is set to "Sealing."

7. Cook for 5 minutes on the "Manual, High Pressure" setting.

8. Once done, carefully open the pot by quick releasing the pressure through the steam valve.

9. Discard most of the brown cooking liquid.

10. Remove the garlic cloves and peel them.

11. Add the lemon juice, tahini, cooked and fresh garlic cloves and pitted black olives to the pot.

12. Using a hand-held immersion blender, process all the ingredients until smooth.

13. Pour out the spread into a serving dish and season with fresh thyme, whole black olives and some extra-virgin olive oil, prior to serving.

Nutrition : 155 Calories; 16.8g Carbohydrates; 11.7g Fat

Carrot Hummus

Preparation Time : 15 minutes

Cooking Time : 10 minutes

Servings : 2

Ingredients :

- 1 chopped carrot
- 2 oz. cooked chickpeas
- 1 tsp. lemon juice
- 1 tsp. tahini
- 1 tsp. fresh parsley

Directions :

1. Place the carrot and chickpeas in your Pressure Pot.
2. Add a cup of water, seal, cook for 10 minutes on Stew.
3. Depressurize naturally. Blend with the remaining ingredients.

Nutrition : 58 Calories; 8g Carbohydrates; 2g Fat

Vegetable Rice Pilaf

Preparation Time : 5 minutes

Cooking Time : 25 minutes

Servings : 6

Ingredients :

- 1 tablespoon olive oil
- ½ medium yellow onion, diced
- 1 cup uncooked long-grain brown rice
- 2 cloves minced garlic
- ½ teaspoon dried basil
- Salt and pepper
- 2 cups fat-free chicken broth
- 1 cup frozen mixed veggies

Directions :

1. Cook oil in a large skillet over medium heat.
2. Add the onion and sauté for 3 minutes until translucent.
3. Stir in the rice and cook until lightly toasted.
4. Add the garlic, basil, salt, and pepper then stir to combined.
5. Stir in the chicken broth then bring to a boil.
6. Decrease heat and simmer, covered, for 10 minutes.
7. Stir in the frozen veggies then cover and cook for another 10 minutes until heated through. Serve hot.

Nutrition : 90 Calories; 12.6g Carbohydrates; 2.2g Fiber

Curry Roasted Cauliflower Florets

Preparation Time : 5 minutes

Cooking Time : 25 minutes

Servings : 6

Ingredients :

- 8 cups cauliflower florets

- 2 tablespoons olive oil

- 1 teaspoon curry powder

- ½ teaspoon garlic powder

- Salt and pepper

Directions :

1. Prep the oven to 425°F and line a baking sheet with foil.

2. Toss the cauliflower with the olive oil and spread on the baking sheet.

3. Sprinkle with curry powder, garlic powder, salt, and pepper.

4. Roast for 25 minutes or until just tender. Serve hot.

Nutrition : 75 Calories; 7.4g Carbohydrates; 3.5g Fiber

Mushroom Barley Risotto

Preparation Time : 5 minutes

Cooking Time : 25 minutes

Servings : 8

Ingredients :

- 4 cups fat-free beef broth
- 2 tablespoons olive oil
- 1 small onion, diced well
- 2 cloves minced garlic
- 8 ounces thinly sliced mushrooms
- ¼ tsp dried thyme
- Salt and pepper
- 1 cup pearled barley
- ½ cup dry white wine

Directions :

1. Heat the beef broth in a medium saucepan and keep it warm.
2. Heat the oil in a large, deep skillet over medium heat.
3. Add the onions and garlic and sauté for 2 minutes then stir in the mushrooms and thyme.
4. Season with salt and pepper and sauté for 2 minutes more.
5. Add the barley and sauté for 1 minute then pour in the wine.
6. Ladle about ½ cup of beef broth into the skillet and stir well to combine.

7. Cook until most of the broth has been absorbed then add another ladle.

8. Repeat until you have used all of the broth and the barley is cooked to al dente.

9. Season and serve hot.

Nutrition : 155 Calories; 21.9g Carbohydrates; 4.4g Fiber

Braised Summer Squash

Preparation Time : 10 minutes

Cooking Time : 20 minutes

Servings : 6

Ingredients :

- 3 tablespoons olive oil
- 3 cloves minced garlic
- ¼ teaspoon crushed red pepper flakes
- 1-pound summer squash, sliced
- 1-pound zucchini, sliced
- 1 teaspoon dried oregano
- Salt and pepper

Directions :

1. Cook oil in a large skillet over medium heat.
2. Add the garlic and crushed red pepper and cook for 2 minutes.
3. Add the summer squash and zucchini and cook for 15 minutes, stirring often, until just tender.
4. Stir in the oregano then season with salt and pepper to taste. serve hot.

Nutrition : 90 Calories; 6.2g Carbohydrates; 1.8g Fiber

Lemon Garlic Green Beans

Preparation Time : 5 minutes

Cooking Time : 10 minutes

Servings : 6

Ingredients :

- 1 1/2 pounds green beans, trimmed
- 2 tablespoons olive oil
- 1 tablespoon fresh lemon juice
- 2 cloves minced garlic
- Salt and pepper

Directions :

1. Fill a large bowl with ice water and set aside.
2. Bring a pot of salted water to boil then add the green beans.
3. Cook for 3 minutes then drain and immediately place in the ice water.
4. Cool the beans completely then drain them well.
5. Heat the oil in a large skillet over medium-high heat.
6. Add the green beans, tossing to coat, then add the lemon juice, garlic, salt, and pepper.
7. Sauté for 3 minutes until the beans are tender-crisp then serve hot.

Nutrition : Calories 75; Total Fat 4.8g; Saturated Fat 0.7g; Total Carbs 8.5g; Net Carbs 4.6g; Protein 2.1g; Sugar 1.7g; Fiber 3.9g; Sodium 7mg

Brown Rice & Lentil Salad

Preparation Time : 10 minutes

Cooking Time : 10 minutes

Servings : 4

Ingredients :

- 1 cup water
- 1/2 cup instant brown rice
- 2 tablespoons olive oil
- 2 tablespoons red wine vinegar
- 1 tablespoon Dijon mustard
- 1 tablespoon minced onion
- 1/2 teaspoon paprika
- Salt and pepper
- 1 (15-ounce) can brown lentils, rinsed and drained
- 1 medium carrot, shredded
- 2 tablespoons fresh chopped parsley

Directions :

1. Stir together the water and instant brown rice in a medium saucepan.
2. Bring to a boil then simmer for 10 minutes, covered.
3. Remove from heat and set aside while you prepare the salad.
4. Whisk together the olive oil, vinegar, Dijon mustard, onion, paprika, salt, and pepper in a medium bowl.
5. Toss in the cooked rice, lentils, carrots, and parsley.

6. Adjust seasoning to taste then stir well and serve warm.

Nutrition : Calories 145; Total Fat 7.7g; Saturated Fat 1g; Total Carbs 13.1g; Net Carbs 10.9g; Protein 6g; Sugar 1g; Fiber 2.2g; Sodium 57mg

Mashed Butternut Squash

Preparation Time : 5 minutes

Cooking Time : 25 minutes

Servings : 6

Ingredients :

- 3 pounds whole butternut squash (about 2 medium)
- 2 tablespoons olive oil
- Salt and pepper

Directions :

1. Preheat the oven to 400F and line a baking sheet with parchment.
2. Cut the squash in half and remove the seeds.
3. Cut the squash into cubes and toss with oil then spread on the baking sheet.
4. Roast for 25 minutes until tender then place in a food processor.
5. Blend smooth then season with salt and pepper to taste.

Nutrition : Calories 90; Total Fat 4.8g; Saturated Fat 0.7g; Total Carbs 12.3g; Net Carbs 10.2g; Protein 1.1g; Sugar 2.3g; Fiber 2.1g; Sodium 4mg

Cilantro Lime Quinoa

Preparation Time : 5 minutes

Cooking Time : 25 minutes

Servings : 6

Ingredients :

- 1 cup uncooked quinoa
- 1 tablespoon olive oil
- 1 medium yellow onion, diced
- 2 cloves minced garlic
- 1 (4-ounce) can diced green chiles, drained
- 1 1/2 cups fat-free chicken broth
- ¾ cup fresh chopped cilantro
- 1/2 cup sliced green onion
- 2 tablespoons lime juice
- Salt and pepper

Directions :

1. Rinse the quinoa thoroughly in cool water using a fine mesh sieve.

2. Heat the oil in a large saucepan over medium heat.

3. Add the onion and sauté for 2 minutes then stir in the chile and garlic.

4. Cook for 1 minute then stir in the quinoa and chicken broth.

5. Bring to a boil then reduce heat and simmer, covered, until the quinoa absorbs the liquid – about 20 to 25 minutes.

6. Remove from heat then stir in the cilantro, green onions, and lime juice.

7. Season with salt and pepper to taste and serve hot.

Nutrition : Calories 150; Total Fat 4.1g; Saturated Fat 0.5g; Total Carbs 22.5g; Net Carbs 19.8g; Protein 6g; Sugar 1.7g; Fiber 2.7g; Sodium 179mg

Oven-Roasted Veggies

Preparation Time : 5 minutes

Cooking Time : 25 minutes

Servings : 6

Ingredients :

- 1 pound cauliflower florets
- 1/2-pound broccoli florets
- 1 large yellow onion, cut into chunks
- 1 large red pepper, cored and chopped
- 2 medium carrots, peeled and sliced
- 2 tablespoons olive oil
- 2 tablespoons apple cider vinegar
- Salt and pepper

Directions :

1. Preheat the oven to 425F and line a large rimmed baking sheet with parchment.
2. Spread the veggies on the baking sheet and drizzle with oil and vinegar.
3. Toss well and season with salt and pepper.
4. Spread the veggies in a single layer then roast for 20 to 25 minutes, stirring every 10 minutes, until tender.
5. Adjust seasoning to taste and serve hot.

Nutrition : Calories 100; Total Fat 5g; Saturated Fat 0.7g; Total Carbs 12.4g; Net Carbs 8.2g; Protein 3.2g; Sugar 5.5g; Fiber 4.2g; Sodium 51mg

Parsley Tabbouleh

Preparation Time : 5 minutes

Cooking Time : 25 minutes

Servings : 6

Ingredients :

- 1 cup water
- 1/2 cup bulgur
- ¼ cup fresh lemon juice
- 2 tablespoons olive oil
- 2 cloves minced garlic
- Salt and pepper
- 2 cups fresh chopped parsley
- 2 medium tomatoes, died
- 1 small cucumber, diced
- ¼ cup fresh chopped mint

Directions :

1. Bring the water and bulgur to a boil in a small saucepan then remove from heat.
2. Cover and let stand until the water are fully absorbed, about 25 minutes.
3. Meanwhile, whisk together the lemon juice, olive oil, garlic, salt, and pepper in a medium bowl.
4. Toss in the cooked bulgur along with the parsley, tomatoes, cucumber, and mint.
5. Season with salt and pepper to taste and serve.

<u>*Nutrition*</u> : Calories 110; Total Fat 5.3g; Saturated Fat 0.9g; Total Carbs 14.4g; Net Carbs 10.5g; Protein 3g; Sugar 2.4g; Fiber 3.9g; Sodium 21mg

Garlic Sautéed Spinach

Preparation Time : 5 minutes

Cooking Time : 10 minutes

Servings : 4

Ingredients :

- 1 1/2 tablespoons olive oil
- 4 cloves minced garlic
- 6 cups fresh baby spinach
- Salt and pepper

Directions :

1. Heat the oil in a large skillet over medium-high heat.
2. Add the garlic and cook for 1 minute.
3. Stir in the spinach and season with salt and pepper.
4. Sauté for 1 to 2 minutes until just wilted. Serve hot.

Nutrition : Calories 60; Total Fat 5.5g; Saturated Fat 0.8g; Total Carbs 2.6g; Net Carbs 1.5g; Protein 1.5g; Sugar 0.2g; Fiber 1.1g; Sodium 36mg

French Lentils

Preparation Time : 5 minutes

Cooking Time : 25 minutes

Servings : 10

Ingredients :

- 2 tablespoons olive oil

- 1 medium onion, diced

- 1 medium carrot, peeled and diced

- 2 cloves minced garlic

- 5 1/2 cups water

- 2 ¼ cups French lentils, rinsed and drained

- 1 teaspoon dried thyme

- 2 small bay leaves

- Salt and pepper

Directions :

1. Heat the oil in a large saucepan over medium heat.

2. Add the onions, carrot, and garlic and sauté for 3 minutes.

3. Stir in the water, lentils, thyme, and bay leaves – season with salt.

4. Bring to a boil then reduce to a simmer and cook until tender, about 20 minutes.

5. Drain any excess water and adjust seasoning to taste. Serve hot.

Nutrition : Calories 185; Total Fat 3.3g; Saturated Fat 0.5g; Total Carbs 27.9; Net Carbs 14.2g; Protein 11.4g; Sugar 1.7g; Fiber 13.7g; Sodium 11mg

Grain-Free Berry Cobbler

Preparation Time : 5 minutes

Cooking Time : 25 minutes

Servings : 10

Ingredients :

- 4 cups fresh mixed berries
- 1/2 cup ground flaxseed
- ¼ cup almond meal
- ¼ cup unsweetened shredded coconut
- 1/2 tablespoon baking powder
- 1 teaspoon ground cinnamon
- ¼ teaspoon salt
- Powdered stevia, to taste
- 6 tablespoons coconut oil

Directions :

1. Preheat the oven to 375F and lightly grease a 10-inch cast-iron skillet.
2. Spread the berries on the bottom of the skillet.
3. Whisk together the dry ingredients in a mixing bowl.
4. Cut in the coconut oil using a fork to create a crumbled mixture.
5. Spread the crumble over the berries and bake for 25 minutes until hot and bubbling.
6. Cool the cobbler for 5 to 10 minutes before serving.

Nutrition : Calories 215; Total Fat 16.8g; Saturated Fat 10.4g; Total Carbs 13.1g; Net Carbs 6.7g; Protein 3.7g; Sugar 5.3g; Fiber 6.4g; Sodium 61mg

Coffee-Steamed Carrots

Preparation Time : 10 minutes

Cooking Time : 3 minutes

Servings : 4

Ingredients :

- 1 cup brewed coffee
- 1 teaspoon light brown sugar
- ½ teaspoon kosher salt
- Freshly ground black pepper
- 1-pound baby carrots
- Chopped fresh parsley
- 1 teaspoon grated lemon zest

Directions :

1. Pour the coffee into the electric pressure cooker. Stir in the brown sugar, salt, and pepper. Add the carrots.
2. Close the pressure cooker. Set to sealing.
3. Cook on high pressure for minutes.
4. Once complete, click Cancel and quick release the pressure.
5. Once the pin drops, open and remove the lid.
6. Using a slotted spoon, portion carrots to a serving bowl. Topped with the parsley and lemon zest, and serve.

Nutrition : 51 Calories; 12g Carbohydrates; 4g Fiber

Rosemary Potatoes

Preparation Time : 5 minutes

Cooking Time : 25 minutes

Servings : 2

Ingredients :

- 1lb red potatoes
- 1 cup vegetable stock
- 2tbsp olive oil
- 2tbsp rosemary sprigs

Directions :

1. Situate potatoes in the steamer basket and add the stock into the Pressure Pot.

2. Steam the potatoes in your Pressure Pot for 15 minutes.

3. Depressurize and pour away the remaining stock.

4. Set to sauté and add the oil, rosemary, and potatoes.

5. Cook until brown.

Nutrition : Per serving: 195 Calories; 31g Carbohydrates; 1g Fat

Corn on the Cob

Preparation Time : 10 minutes

Cooking Time : 5 minutes

Servings : 12

Ingredients :

- 6 ears corn

Directions :

1. Take off husks and silk from the corn. Cut or break each ear in half.

2. Pour 1 cup of water into the bottom of the electric pressure cooker. Insert a wire rack or trivet.

3. Place the corn upright on the rack, cut-side down. Seal lid of the pressure cooker.

4. Cook on high pressure for 5 minutes.

5. When its complete, select Cancel and quick release the pressure.

6. When pin drops, unlock and take off lid.

7. Pull out the corn from the pot. Season as desired and serve immediately.

Nutrition : 62 Calories; 14g Carbohydrates; 1g Fiber

Chili Lime Salmon

Preparation Time : 6 minutes

Cooking Time : 10 minutes

Servings : 2

Ingredients :

For Sauce:

- 1 jalapeno pepper
- 1 tablespoon chopped parsley
- 1 teaspoon minced garlic
- 1/2 teaspoon cumin
- 1/2 teaspoon paprika
- 1/2 teaspoon lime zest
- 1 tablespoon honey
- 1 tablespoon lime juice
- 1 tablespoon olive oil
- 1 tablespoon water

For Fish:

- 2 salmon fillets, each about 5 ounces
- 1 cup water
- 1/2 teaspoon salt
- 1/8 teaspoon ground black pepper

Directions :

1. Prepare salmon and for this, season salmon with salt and black pepper until evenly coated.

2. Plugin Pressure Pot, insert the inner pot, pour in water, then place steamer basket and place seasoned salmon on it.

3. Seal Pressure Pot with its lid, press the 'steam' button, then press the 'timer' to set the cooking time to 5 minutes and cook on high pressure, for 5 minutes.

4. Transfer all the ingredients for the sauce in a bowl, whisk until combined and set aside until required.

5. When the timer beeps, press 'cancel' button and do quick pressure release until pressure nob drops down.

6. Open the Pressure Pot, then transfer salmon to a serving plate and drizzle generously with prepared sauce.

7. Serve straight away.

Nutrition : 305 Calories; 29g Carbohydrates; 6g Fiber

Collard Greens

Preparation Time : 5 minutes

Cooking Time : 6 hours

Servings : 12

Ingredients :

- 2 pounds chopped collard greens
- ¾ cup chopped white onion
- 1 teaspoon onion powder
- 1 teaspoon garlic powder
- 1 teaspoon salt
- 2 teaspoons brown sugar
- ½ teaspoon ground black pepper
- ½ teaspoon red chili powder
- ¼ teaspoon crushed red pepper flakes
- 3 tablespoons apple cider vinegar
- 2 tablespoons olive oil
- 14.5-ounce vegetable broth
- 1/2 cup water

Directions :

1. Plugin Pressure Pot, insert the inner pot, add onion and collard and then pour in vegetable broth and water.

2. Close Pressure Pot with its lid, seal, press the 'slow cook' button, then press the 'timer' to set the cooking time to 6 hours at high heat setting.

3. When the timer beeps, press 'cancel' button and do natural pressure release until pressure nob drops down.

4. Open the Pressure Pot, add remaining ingredients and stir until mixed.

5. Then press the 'sauté/simmer' button and cook for 3 to minutes or more until collards reach to desired texture.

6. Serve straight away.

Nutrition : 49 Calories; 2.3g Carbohydrates; 0.5g Fiber

Mashed Pumpkin

Preparation Time : 9 minutes

Cooking Time : 15 minutes

Servings : 2

Ingredients :

- 2 cups chopped pumpkin
- 0.5 cup water
- 2tbsp powdered sugar-free sweetener of choice
- 1tbsp cinnamon

Directions :

1. Place the pumpkin and water in your Pressure Pot.
2. Seal and cook on Stew 15 minutes.
3. Remove and mash with the sweetener and cinnamon.

Nutrition : 12 Calories; 3g Carbohydrates; 1g Sugar

Parmesan-Topped Acorn Squash

Preparation Time : 8 minutes

Cooking Time : 20 minutes

Servings : 4

Ingredients :

- 1 acorn squash (about 1 pound)
- 1 tablespoon extra-virgin olive oil
- 1 teaspoon dried sage leaves, crumbled
- ¼ teaspoon freshly grated nutmeg
- 1/8 teaspoon kosher salt
- 1/8 teaspoon freshly ground black pepper
- 2 tablespoons freshly grated Parmesan cheese

Directions :

1. Chop acorn squash in half lengthwise and remove the seeds. Cut each half in half for a total of 4 wedges. Snap off the stem if it's easy to do.

2. In a small bowl, combine the olive oil, sage, nutmeg, salt, and pepper. Brush the cut sides of the squash with the olive oil mixture.

3. Fill 1 cup of water into the electric pressure cooker and insert a wire rack or trivet.

4. Place the squash on the trivet in a single layer, skin-side down.

5. Set the lid of the pressure cooker on sealing.

6. Cook on high pressure for 20 minutes.

7. Once done, press Cancel and quick release the pressure.

8. Once the pin drops, open it.

9. Carefully remove the squash from the pot, sprinkle with the Parmesan, and serve.

Nutrition : 85 Calories; 12g Carbohydrates; 2g Fiber

Lightning Source UK Ltd.
Milton Keynes UK
UKHW020811080621
385129UK00001B/66